WORLD WAR II: THE RESISTANCE

The Fight for Freedom in Occupied Europe

Written by Stéphanie Simonnet
Translated by Rebecca Neal

History 50MINUTES.com

THE RESISTANCE DURING THE SECOND WORLD WAR   1

Key information

Introduction

CONTEXT   3

The start of the Second World War

The early stages of the Resistance

Europe under German occupation

SOME KEY FIGURES OF THE *RESISTANCE*   14

France

Poland

Germany

THE RESISTANCE   19

The different forms of resistance

The Resistance in Poland

The Resistance in France

The Resistance in Germany

The question of collaboration

THE SUPPRESSION OF THE RESISTANCE   34

Harsh punishment

Tragic losses for mixed results

SUMMARY   38

FIND OUT MORE   41

THE RESISTANCE DURING THE SECOND WORLD WAR

KEY INFORMATION

- **When:** 1939-1945.
- **Where:** Across almost all of Europe.
- **Context:** The Second World War and German occupation.
- **Some key protagonists:**
  - Charles de Gaulle, French general and statesman (1890-1970).
  - Jean Moulin, French politician and Resistance member (1899-1943).
  - Witold Pilecki, Polish soldier and Resistance member (1901-1948).
  - Libertas Schulze-Boysen, German journalist and Resistance member (1913-1942).
- **Impact:** although the Resistance contributed to the success of various Allied actions to liberate Europe from the Nazi invaders, it sustained extremely heavy losses for sometimes mixed results.

INTRODUCTION

Although the Maquis, distributors of underground newspapers, Gaullist saboteurs and nuns who concealed Jewish children in their convents can all be grouped under the same heading, this only makes describing the movement that brought them together even more complex. Indeed, defining the Resistance is a risky undertaking because participation and experiences varied so much across Nazi-occupied Europe between 1939 and 1945. According to the historian François Bédarida (1926-2001), it is "clandestine action carried out, in the name of the liberty of the nation and the dignity of humanity, by volunteers organised to fight against the domination [...] of their country by a Nazi or fascist regime"[1] (*Vingtième Siècle*, 1986). The advantage of this definition is that it highlights the plurality of the movement. But why did these volunteers choose to join the Resistance? Who were they? What did they do and what were the consequences of their actions?

---

1. This quotation has been translated by 50Minutes.com.

CONTEXT

THE START OF THE SECOND WORLD WAR

The war began on 1 September 1939, after Germany invaded Poland. This event led France and the United Kingdom to go to war against the Axis powers (Nazi Germany, fascist Italy and, from 27 September 1940, the Japanese Empire), in accordance with a mutual military assistance treaty signed with Poland in 1921. In the years that followed, Germany notched up a string of victories against the Allies and seemed invincible. In April 1940, it invaded Denmark and Norway. In May, it was the turn of Luxembourg, Belgium and the Netherlands. In June, the French army was crushed by the Wehrmacht (the German army). In September 1940 and then in April 1941, Hitler (1889-1945) invaded Egypt, Yugoslavia and Greece to support Mussolini's Italy, which was in full rout against these countries. In June, the USSR, which until then had been spared by the Nazi-Soviet Pact (an agreement signed between the Third Reich and the Stalin's Soviet Union concerning neutrality in the case of a conflict between the two parties and the Western powers), was invaded.

Photograph of German troops entering Prague in 1939.

Historians have put forward three main causes for the conflict. First of all, there is the unsatisfactory settlement of the First World War (1914-1918) by peace treaties, in particular the Treaty of Versailles, which gave rise to resentment, frustration and a desire to reconquer territory among the losing parties and some of the victors. Another factor is the impact of the 1929 financial crisis on the weakened economies of the participants in the Great War: unemployment and recession helped fascist nationalists (Italy) and the Nazis (Germany) to rise to power. These groups then implemented rearmament programmes to try to lift their countries out of the slump they found themselves in. Finally, the ideologies of these totalitarian states were in complete opposition to the Allied democracies, which feared the effects of the expansionist and hegemonic ambitions of Italy and Germany.

The Treaty of Versailles, signed on 28 June 1919 by Germany and the Allies following the First World War, attracted a number of criticisms at the time and was not signed by the United States. Indeed, its terms were far too harsh on the losing countries, which made them even more resentful. Germany felt particularly humiliated, especially as it was not even invited to the conferences to draw up the peace agreement.

This treaty, which the Germans labelled a diktat, attributed sole responsibility for the conflict to them and ordered them to pay 132 billion marks in reparations to France and Belgium. Furthermore, the country lost around 25 000 square miles of territory, including Alsace and Lorraine (which it had annexed in 1871), part of Western Prussia, which was transferred to Poland and gave the new country access to the sea via the Danzig Corridor, and all its African colonies. Its military power was also wiped out.

Germany was not the only country hurt by the Treaty of Versailles. Italy, which was on the side of the victors, spoke of a "mutilated victory" as it did not receive the territories it had been promised in the Treaty of London in 1915 (western Istria and Dalmatia).

THE EARLY STAGES OF THE RESISTANCE

In Warsaw on 27 September 1939, 26 days after the invasion of Poland by the Wehrmacht, the Polish army was defeated. In response to the tremendous brutality of the German occupiers, General Michał Tadeusz Karaszewicz-Tokarzewski (1893-1964) established an underground army, which would become the *Armia Krajowa* (Home Army) on 14 February 1942. As the armed wing of the Polish government in exile in France, its main aim was to liberate the country by preparing for a national uprising to accompany the actions of the Allies.

DID YOU KNOW?

The Polish army was the largest underground resistance organisation during the Second World War. It provided the Allies with crucial information on the Eastern Front and secret German weapons. It also organised resistance on the ground, carrying out many acts of sabotage and destroying German supply trains and communication points.

A few months later, on 18 June 1940, thousands of miles away on the Western Front, General Charles de Gaulle was at the BBC to record a message to the French people. He solemnly appealed to the French to continue their fight against the German enemy: "Whatever happens, the flame of the French resistance not must not be extinguished and will not be extinguished" (cited by The Lehrman Institute).

Although one in two French households owned a wireless, only a portion of the population was able to listen to the radio on 18 June, as the rest had been plunged into the chaos of the exodus. However, the message circulated thanks to word-of-mouth and the following day several newspapers published excerpts of the appeal, which de Gaulle would repeat on the radio on the 19 and 22 June.

The 18 June appeal.

However, confusion prevailed in the country. Two days earlier, on 16 June, Marshal Pétain (1856-1951), the great victor of the Battle of Verdun (21 February-19 December 1916) had taken power and proposed signing an armistice with Hitler's Germany. Indeed, in the spring of 1940 France found itself trapped: the Wehrmacht was on the Loire and between 7 and 8 million French citizens had fled south to escape the German advance, followed by soldiers who were fleeing and had been stripped of their command.

EUROPE UNDER GERMAN OCCUPATION

From 1941, with the invasion of the Balkans and the USSR, almost all of Europe was under German domination and was therefore forced to put its human resources and economic capacities at the disposal of the Third Reich in order to support its war effort. The situation of the occupied countries differed considerably depending on the objective of the Nazis, whose plans were largely based on the racist ideology developed by Hitler.

Hitler's ideology

The main principles of the Nazi ideology set out by Hitler in his book *Mein Kampf* (*My Struggle*), published in 1925-1926, are based on the slogan *Ein Volk, ein Reich, ein Führer* (One people, one empire, one leader). The German people, who Hitler considered superior, allegedly descended from the Aryans and were at the top of the classification of races. The Germans should gather themselves around their leader, Hitler, to better ensure their domination over other, inferior, races and to conquer the space they needed, *Lebensraum* (living space). In this classification, Jews and Slavs were judged to be *untermenschen* (subhuman), destined to be annihilated or enslaved.

The Führer considered the dominated countries to the East as part of the German living space, and thought that they needed to be 'emptied' of their population in order for colonisers to settle there. In Poland, Yugoslavia and the USSR, there were massacres and looting from the first days of the invasion. Populations were often deported and dispossessed of their lands in favour of the Germans. From September 1939, the *Einsatzgruppen* (task forces) killed 20 000 people in Poland. In June 1941, 600 000 hectares in the USSR were seized by the SS (*Schutzstaffel*, literally 'protection squadron') and more than 2 million civilians were forcibly transferred to Germany and placed in work camps, where conditions were extremely difficult.

Conversely, in the West the Nazis did not follow the logic of extermination, but pillaged regions and sowed terror. Once a country had been conquered, the Germans claimed war spoils. As such, in Norway, Belgium, France and the Netherlands, the armies were forced to hand over weapons, munitions, means of transport and communications to the Wehrmacht. The countries were also forced to give the Germans money, which amounted to 400 million francs per day in France.

DID YOU KNOW?

Nazi Germany, which had very little gold and cash before the war, put in place a bartering system between countries in 1940. This system, known as 'clearing', allowed it to acquire supplies on credit form the occupied countries. At the end of the war in 1945, German debt stood at an estimated 16.2 billion marks. It would be reduced to 7.5 billion following an agreement reached in London on 27 February 1953 between the FDR (Federal Republic of Germany) and the Allies, who wanted to boost the German economy.

However, the looting was not only financial: it was also human. Between 1939 and 1945, around 400 000 Belgians and 650 000 French citizens were requisitioned for compulsory work service and moved to Germany to work in factories and farms, along with prisoners of war (around 2 million men). Consequently, there was a marked reduction in the workforce in Western Europe. In addition, there were shortages of vital commodities (food, fuel, textiles, household products, etc.). Between June 1940 and June 1944, the Germans requisitioned 2.8 million tonnes of wheat (half the annual harvest), 845 000 tonnes of meat (more than the consumption of 40 million French inhabitants during 1941), 711 000 tonnes of potatoes and 220 million eggs from France.

Furthermore, the majority of the occupied countries were forced to introduce rationing. Each inhabitant had a card which they could use to obtain a certain amount of food, clothing, etc., determined according to their needs. Even so, purchase was not guaranteed, and people had to join huge queues outside shops, which formed well before they opened. Every day, signs appeared as early as the morning announcing shortages of basic commodities, such as bread and meat. Coal and petrol essentially ran out: often, the population had to limit themselves to just heating one room of their housing during the harsh winters of the occupation, and travel by train, by bicycle or on foot instead of driving. Cards were also necessary to obtain clothing and shoes, but fabric and leather were rare. This is why most old items of clothing were used to create others and shoes were repaired by nailing wooden soles onto them.

How much to survive?

In France in 1943, an adolescent received 30 grams of meat, 7 grams of cheese and 150 grams of potatoes per day. In 2015, the average daily consumption for adolescents was 250 grams of meat, 300 grams of potatoes and around 40 grams of cheese. It is clear that the rations provided during the war were insufficient, and inhabitants needed to find solutions to make their daily lives more bearable. Unobtainable products were replaced by substitutes: saccharin was used as sugar; Jerusalem artichokes and swedes, which had previously been reserved for livestock, replaced vegetables; and roasted barley or acorns replaced coffee. Those who could afford it purchased meat, dairy products and clothing on the black market at exorbitant prices: up to 600 francs for a kilo of butter, which officially cost 79 francs before the war, and 110 francs for a dozen eggs, which officially cost 36 francs. Between 1940 and

1944, the Vichy regime filed over a million reports as part of a crackdown on the black market, which was the most widespread form of delinquency during that period. Rulebreakers were taken to court and risked up to 2 years in prison and a 100 000 franc fine (law dated 21 October 1940).

However, living under German control did not just mean being cold and hungry and surviving in difficult material conditions: it also meant living in an atmosphere of intimidation, fuelled by fear. In order to keep a close eye on the population and limit underground activities linked to the Resistance, a curfew banned people from going out at night between 10pm and 6am, and residents needed an *Ausweis* (pass) to move through some strictly controlled areas. All gatherings were outlawed, and papers were checked frequently. The media and culture were censored in order to turn them into German propaganda tools. In July 1940, the Germans requisitioned Radio France, which broadcast all over Europe, causing the BBC to adopt "Radio France lies, Radio France lies, Radio France is German" as the slogan over the opening credits of its programme in France. In the programme, they would then include some coded messages addressed to the Resistance.

This picture of German occupation in Europe allows us to understand why some members of the population joined the Resistance. Although the risks meant that there were not many of them, the members of the Resistance were men and women of all ages, from varying social backgrounds, with different political, philosophical and religious leanings.

SOME KEY FIGURES OF THE *RESISTANCE*

FRANCE

Charles de Gaulle

Charles de Gaulle, a general who took part in the Battle of France in May 1940, was opposed to any peace with Germany. Consequently, when Pétain requested an armistice, de Gaulle opted to go into exile in England to continue the fight. He issued his famous appeal on 18 June, and worked for four years to unify the French Resistance. His aim was to earn recognition for these movements so that they would become the legitimate representatives of France for the Allies. In 1943, with the help of Jean Moulin, he founded the National Council of the Resistance, which brought together all the resistance movements and coordinated the fight against Nazi occupation and the Vichy government. At the same time, he organised the liberation of the country and provided France with a government in exile, the *Comité national français*, which would later become the provisional government of the French Republic upon liberation (June 1944-May 1945) and would be recognised by the Allies. On 26 August 1944, during the liberation of Paris, he made a triumphant return, marching down the Champs-Élysées and delivering a famous speech: "Paris outraged! Paris broken! Paris martyred! But Paris liberated!" On 3 September 1944, he became the leader of the provisional government and helped to re-establish democracy in France.

Photograph of de Gaulle's triumphant return to Paris, 26 August 1944.

Jean Moulin

After being dismissed from his post as prefect of the Eure-et-Loir department by the Vichy government, Jean Moulin decided to join Free France in London in September 1941. He was received by de Gaulle and informed him of the state of the Resistance in France and its financial and material needs. De Gaulle then sent him to Lyon to unify the Resistance movements. In Lyon, he managed to set up a genuine underground administration and became the main intermediary between the internal Resistance and de Gaulle, whose authority he ensured recognition for. On 27 May 1943, he organised and chaired the first National

Council of the Resistance, which brought together the leaders of all the French Resistance groups. In June of that year,
he was arrested in Caluire-et-Cuire, a suburb of Lyon, and
taken to the Gestapo headquarters. He was tortured and
died of his injuries on the train taking him to Germany on
8 July 1943. In 1964, the 20th anniversary of the liberation of
France, a memorial was dedicated to him in the Panthéon.

POLAND

Witold Pilecki

At the start of the war, Witold Pilecki was an officer in the
Polish army which was fighting the Wehrmacht. In November
1939, he created one of the first Resistance organisations in
his country. On 19 September 1940, he deliberately allowed
himself to be captured by the Germans in the streets of
Warsaw and was immediately sent to Auschwitz. He aimed
to collect information on the activities of the Germans to
pass on to the Polish Resistance, and to organise a Resistance
network within the camp itself. He also managed to create a
radio transmitter and smuggle in medication, and infected
members of the SS with typhus by using lice. In October
1940, he sent his first report to Warsaw, which was passed
on to the British government in 1941 in the hope that the
Allies would drop arms into Auschwitz. In April 1943, having
realised that the Allies would not intervene, he decided to
escape to personally convince his superiors to attack the
camp. However, the *Armia Krajowa* was not big enough.
After liberation, he went on to fight against the dictatorship
established in his country by the Soviets, who sentenced
him to death and shot him in 1948.

GERMANY

Libertas Schulze-Boysen

Libertas Schulze-Boysen was the wife of the first lieutenant Harro Schulze-Boysen (1909-1942), an employee of the Reich Air Transport Ministry. Along with Arvid Harnack (1901-1942), a scientific adviser to the government, the couple helped found an organisation bringing together some 100 opponents of the Third Reich and the war. Libertas used her job at the Reich Propaganda Ministry to gather information on Nazi war crimes and inform the German people about them through leaflets and posters. From 1941, the couple were in contact with a Soviet agent and passed information to the USSR, including the Wehrmacht's plan to attack the country imminently. At the end of 1942, the organisation was dismantled by the Gestapo, which labelled it the *Rote Kapelle* (Red Orchestra). Libertas, her husband and 50 other people were sentenced to death and executed in Berlin.

THE RESISTANCE

During the war, the majority of the states in Europe broke down and institutions progressively disappeared. Unfortunately, to get out of the impasse, they could not count on a tradition of resistance, apart from Poland, which had a long legacy of national struggle and, to a certain extent, France and Belgium, which had been occupied during the Great War. Those who decided to resist were initially isolated, but ended up becoming organised as time went on.

THE DIFFERENT FORMS OF RESISTANCE

The Resistance was based around three main modes of action. First of all, there was civilian resistance, through which the population demonstrated their refusal to see their country occupied. This action could be individual, for example listening to radio stations broadcast from London, producing counter-propaganda (graffiti, the defacing of Nazi or collaborationist posters, the production and distribution of clandestine publications such as leaflets, newspapers and cartoons) or refusing to carry out the orders of the administration.

THE ROLE OF THE RADIO IN CIVILIAN RESISTANCE

Radio Londres was a series of radio programmes broadcast by the BBC in French from 19 June 1940, encouraging insurrection against the occupier. It quickly gained a massive audience in spite of potential sanctions which ranged from the confiscation of radio equipment and fines of between 200 and 10 000 francs to imprisonment and even deportation. To avoid being caught, listeners had to be careful when listening to broadcasts and hid their radio sets in partition walls, cupboards and pans when they were not listening to them.

In 1941, after the German air offensive against England had been defeated, an underground radio host from the Belgian government in exile in London suggested that his compatriots draw a V for Victory on the walls to symbolise their support for their English allies. The appeal was a success: towns and cities across Belgium and France, and then all of Europe, were covered with this sign, which irritated collaborationist governments and the Germans, who sought to punish those responsible.

AVIS IMPORTANT.

PENDANT la nuit de Samedi à Dimanche les 28 et 29 Juin 1941 un écriteau militaire allemand fut défiguré et la lettre " V " et autres écrits furent peint sur certaines maisons ainsi que sur des murs et dans la route dans le district du Rouge Bouillon, en la paroisse de St. Hélier.

Nous avons été informés par le Commandant d'Etape que cela constituait de sérieux actes de sabotage et à moins que le ou les coupables se présentent ou soient découverts avant midi demain (Jeudi) le 3 Juillet 1941, les sanctions suivantes seront imposées par le Commandant d'Etapes :

1. Les habitants du district sont appelés à fournir une garde civile de nuit pour éviter le renouvellement de pareils actes.

2. Tous les appareils de radiophonie appartenant aux occupants de ce district seront confisqués, et

3. Une amende sera imposée sur les habitants du district.

Le district affecté est cette portion urbaine des paroisses de St. Hélier et St. Sauveur, située approximativement au Nord de Roussel Street, Great Union Road, Windsor Road, Val Plaisant à Victoria Street, puis Victoria Street, Stopford et St. Saviour's Road.

Ceux pouvant donner des informations qui permettront de découvrir le ou les auteurs des actes en question sont requis de communiquer immédiatement avec le Connétable de St. Hélier ou le Chef de Police de St. Sauveur.

C. W. DURET AUBIN,
Procureur-Général,

C. J. CUMING,
Connétable de St. Hélier.

G. J. MOURANT,
Chef de Police de St. Sauveur.

St. Hélier,
Ce 1er Juillet 1941.

Public notice announcing the measures taken to put an end to this resistance campaign in the Rouge Bouillon area of St. Helier, Jersey on 1 July 1941.

This resistance could also be collective and take the form of popular gatherings in public spaces for patriotic reasons or as civil disobedience. On 14 July 1942, in several major cities in unoccupied France (Lyon, Marseille, Toulouse, Grenoble, etc.), thousands of people marched before war memorials and in squares, displaying the red, white and blue flag and playing the Marseillaise. On 30 April and 1 May 1943, 500 000 Dutch workers went on strike against the Compulsory Work Service, which allowed 300 000 men to escape this measure.

There was also a resistance that was organised into networks, which first focused on information and escape channels, then on armed struggle. From London, the British authorities and the governments in exile sent agents to recruit volunteers in the occupied countries in order to collect information on the enemy. More than 1 million Poles had been requisitioned, and they proved particularly effective at this task: between 1939 and 1945, they produced over half the reports reaching London, and it was thanks to them that the British leadership found out in 1942 about the German V-1 missiles that would be used against the United Kingdom between June 1944 and March 1945. In addition to information, it was necessary to organise escape channels from September 1939. Andrée de Jongh (Belgian Resistance member, 1916-2007) was responsible for the Comet Line, which allowed over 700 war volunteers, Resistance members and Allied soldiers, including 288 aviators, to escape or hide between 1941 and the liberation. At the same time, there were an increasing number of bombings and acts of sabotage in Europe: railway lines, bridges and roads were blown up; action was taken in the factories to slow down production or damage goods intended for the occu-pier; and Nazi officers were killed. This was all done in spite of increasing repression with, in particular, the application of a hostage policy: one attack against the occupier would lead to the mass execution of civilians. On the night of 1 to 2 April 1944, a railway line was sabotaged, which stopped a train transporting a battalion of an SS armoured division to Ascq (northern France). The attack only inflicted material damage, but the battalion commander ordered the rounding up and execution of 86 civilians from the village. This incident raised strong emotions and reopened the controversy over the effectiveness of this kind of action, leading some members of the Resistance to adopt a wait-and-see approach.

Finally, there was a kind of resistance that can be described as humanitarian, with the primary aim of helping the victims of repression and Nazi and collaborationist persecution. This support was notably given to escaped prisoners of war, those who defied the Compulsory Work Service, and Jews, who were in great danger.

In the East, in Poland and above all in urban areas, from 1940 onwards the Germans stripped Jews of their possessions, herded them into ghettos, the most notorious of which was the Warsaw Ghetto, and forced them to work in the armaments industry. Following the Wannsee Conference (20 January 1942) in Berlin, the Nazis organised the systematic extermination of the Jews. Six death camps (Auschwitz, Bełżec, Chełmno, Majdanek, Sobibor and Treblinka) were built in Poland in order to kill millions of Jews from Poland and the rest of Europe. An estimated 89.5% of Poland's Jewish population was exterminated in this way.

Photograph of Jewish prisoners reduced to slavery in the Buchenwald concentration camp taken during the Liberation, 16 April 1945.

In the West, the Germans and collaborationist govern-ments adopted discriminatory policies. Jews were forced to register themselves (which would then make it easier to round up and deport them), banned from working in certain 'sensitive' sectors (the press, public service, teaching, the medical professions, etc.) and visiting some public spaces, and obligated to wear a distinguishing symbol (the yellow star).

Photograph of a roundup during the Warsaw Ghetto Uprising.

Members of the Resistance helped the victims of anti-Jewish persecution by providing them with accommodation, hiding places, money, clothing and food cards. In addition, false document laboratories were created, priests offered to provide false baptism certificates, and thousands of children were taken in by non-Jewish families. Escape channels to neighbouring countries, such as Switzerland and Spain, were also established. This assistance mobilised many people, including the Catholic and Protestant Churches, which played a large part in this rescue effort and even publicly protested against persecution. In July 1942, Catholic bishops and Protestant leaders in the Netherlands sent a telegram to the commissioner of the Reich (who represented the Nazi authorities in the Netherlands) denouncing the Nazis' unjust and cruel treatment of the Jews. The text was then read in Catholic and Protestant churches. In retaliation, the commissioner ordered the arrest and deportation of Jews who had converted to Catholicism and worsened living conditions for the Dutch, who he thought he could make agree with Nazi ideas.

Each national Resistance movement had its own characteristics depending on the situation of the country, the conditions of the occupation and the aid provided by the Allies, which generally remained limited. Indeed, the Allies did not recognise the Resistance movements as a real force in the fight against the Germans until very late. They were also often mistrustful and scornful of these armed men who lacked real legitimacy. Furthermore, there were divisions within national Resistance movements, between Communists and non-Communists, and between those who advised armed direct action and those who favoured information, propaganda and escape while waiting for the Allies to intervene. This was not at all conducive to action on the ground. In Yugoslavia, these political, ideological and ethnic oppositions led to civil war between the Chetnik resistance members of Draža Mihailović (Serb general, 1893-1946), a Serbian royalist group, and supporters of Tito (politician and soldier, 1892-1980), who were Communists and Yugoslavs.

THE RESISTANCE IN POLAND

The reason that the largest underground Resistance movement, the *Armia Krajowa*, emerged in Poland is that the

Polish people had previously rebelled on several occasions throughout their history, in particular following the dividing up of their territory in the 18th century. Nationalist and patriotic sentiment was particularly developed there. The aim of this domestic army, which was formed by the Polish government in exile in France then London, was to liberate the national territory. It was active between September 1939 and January 1945 and had between 50 000 and 350 000 members spread across 60 regional branches. In spite of difficulties getting hold of weapons and equipment (only some tens of thousands of Resistance members were armed), it managed to implement a project of intense military and economic sabotage. It was responsible for thousands of raids and hundreds of acts of sabotage on the railways. It also did not hesitate to directly attack the Wehrmacht. Its main military operations include the Warsaw Uprising (1 August – 2 October 1944). During this episode, 46 000 members of the Resistance and 200 000 civilian sympathisers rose up against the German occupiers as part of the national military plan *Burza* ('Storm' in English), with the aim of preserving the sovereignty of the country in the face of the Red Army advance. After 63 days of fierce war in the streets, the uprising was finally put down by SS regiments. 18 000 members of the Polish Resistance and 150 000 civilians were killed, 25 000 people were wounded and 350 000 were deported. In addition, up to 85% of the city was razed to the ground. As well as military operations, the *Armia Krajowa* carried out an intense propaganda campaign and established an extensive intelligence network.

In parallel with the military resistance, the Polish government in exile in London organised and supported a cultural resistance. From 1942, teachers put in place underground education groups known as *komplety* in order to resist Nazi plans to eradicate Polish culture. Almost 2 million pupils benefitted from this teaching, which ranged from primary school to university level, in spite of the fact that both teachers and students were risking death.

THE RESISTANCE IN FRANCE

France's situation during the war was unique. The country was divided between a zone occupied by the Germans (northern half and Atlantic coast) and a free zone (southern half), but the entire French territory was governed by Marshal Pétain, who practised a policy of collaboration with the Nazis. Consequently, members of the Resistance were fighting against both the German occupier and the Vichy regime.

Although they were not very developed in the beginning, the movements grew and became structured thanks to events which led to and strengthened the involvement of a greater number of individuals, such as the invasion of the USSR by Nazi Germany (June 1941), which reinforced the determination of Communists in the Resistance, or the establishment of the Compulsory Work Service in France (September 1942), which led many people who were against this measure to join the Resistance in order to oppose it.

In both zones, the *Combat*, *Franc-Tireur*, *Libération-Nord*, *Ceux de la Résistance* and *National Front* groups, to cite only the best-known examples, emerged. Historians apparently recorded 268 such groups, a proportion of which remain largely unknown. In 1943, thanks to the work of Charles de Gaulle and Jean Moulin, the internal resistance was unified under the National Council of the Resistance, which brought together representatives of movements in both zones, political parties and trade unions. On 15 March 1945, the Council adopted a programme which included an immediate plan of action with the aim of liberating the country, and the measures to be applied after liberation to re-establish republican legality (democracy, universal suffrage, freedom of the press, etc.) and promote major economic and social reforms.

THE RESISTANCE IN GERMANY

Internal resistance to Nazism, which for a long time was not widely known about outside Germany, involved a handful of unarmed and isolated individuals within a Nazified society where any attempt at opposition was swiftly silenced. From 1933, the year of Hitler's rise to power, onwards, 700 000 Germans who were considered to be opponents of the regime were sent to concentration camps. Resistance members came above all from communist, socialist and Christian circles. The intervention of the Catholic and Protestant Churches notably forced the Nazis to abandon the *Aktion T4* involuntary euthanasia programme, at least officially. On 9 July 1940, the Protestant pastor Theophil Wurm (1868-1953) wrote a letter to the Nazi Minister of the Interior condemning the this "illegal and immoral programme of mass murder"[2] (Kershaw, 2008).

Another resistance organisation in Germany was the White Rose, which was very active in spite of the fact that its core group was made up of just five students from Munich, including a very young woman, Sophie Scholl. All five were beheaded for writing and distributing leaflets intended to awaken the German collective conscience to the Nazi regime.

THE QUESTION OF COLLABORATION

Just as there were several forms of resistance, there were also several forms of collaboration. First of all, there were the collaborationists who cooperated fully with the Nazi occupiers, approved of their principles and ideals and wanted them to win: this was the case in Norway under Quisling (nominal head of government during Nazi occupation,

---

2. This quotation has been translated by 50Minutes.com.

1887-1945), Hungary under Horthy (admiral and regent of the Kingdom of Hungary, a German ally, 1868-1957), and in some political parties, such as that of Léon Degrelle (Belgian politician, 1906-1994) in Wallonia. Alongside these were collaborationist countries which chose to cooperate militarily and economically with the Nazi occupier, without necessarily agreeing with all aspects of their ideology, in order to preserve their country's interests. This was notably the case for the Vichy government in France. Others, such as the Netherlands and Belgium, whose governments had fled to London, practised a neutral collaboration, meaning that their administrations resigned themselves to working with Germany because they had no other choice, but did not share the political and ideological principles of Nazism.

On a personal level, the civilian population could also choose to serve the occupier, out of either conviction or ambition. As such, some inhabitants of occupied countries maintained friendly personal relationships with the Germans, informed on people they knew in letters to the Gestapo (an average of at least 2700 letters per day in France), solicited orders from the enemy (in the case of business owners), and had professional or romantic relationships with German soldiers, etc. These actions have been described as "everyday collaboration".

DID YOU KNOW?

Between 20 000 and 40 000 women who were accused, wrongly or rightly, of collaborating with the German occupier had their heads shaved in France between 1944 and the end of 1945. Whether this was 'horizontal' collaboration (which included sexual relations between the Nazis and some women) or more classic forms of collaboration (informing, spying, participation in various operations, etc.), the guilty parties received the same humiliating punishment: shaving. These were real performances which took place in front of a jeering crowd outside a place representing French republicanism, such as the town hall or the prefecture. The woman could then be paraded through the town or city. Historians claim that between 100 000 and 200 000 children resulted from relationships between French women and German soldiers.

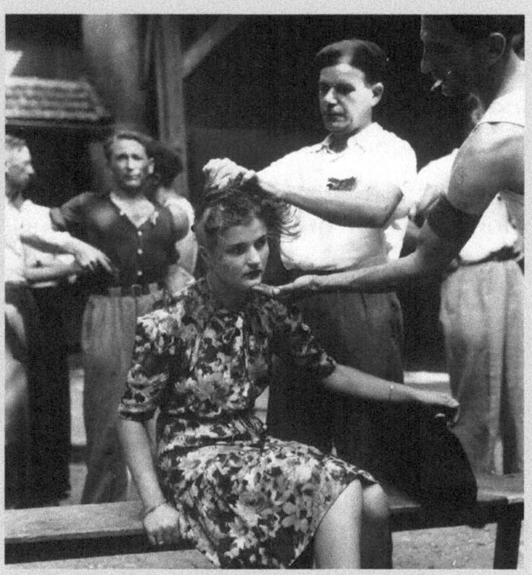

Photograph of a woman having her head shaved in Montélimar, August 1944.

THE SUPPRESSION OF
THE RESISTANCE

HARSH PUNISHMENT

Anyone who participated in the Resistance lived in constant fear of being discovered, arrested, tortured, imprisoned, deported or executed. However, members of the Resistance also had the fate of their organisation in their hands. If they were arrested, their organisation could fall. Everyone had to keep their guard up because their organisation could be infiltrated by Nazi spies. In 1943, the French intelligence network *Alliance*, which had 3000 members, was infiltrated by an agent from the *Abwehr* (a Germany military intelligence organisation). Subsequently, 1000 people were arrested and 413 were deported or executed, leaving just 80 agents after the roundup. In most countries across Europe, acts of resistance were swiftly repressed by the occupier to preserve order. Two forms of action were particularly targeted: spying and armed struggle. To do this, the Germans could count on the help of some governments which had chosen to collaborate.

In this respect, the Vichy government offered a greater degree of police collaboration than had been set out in the armistice, hoping in this way to secure a better place for the country in German-occupied Europe. 113 000 police officers and 150 000 militiamen were put in service of the Nazis as part of the repression. This cooperation was made official with the signing of the *accords Oberg-Bousquet* in August 1942. Although repression was initially carried out primarily by judicial means, the proliferation of Resistance movements from summer 1941 onwards led to a toughening of the repression, with an increase in arrests and death sentences, the systematisation of judicial deportation and the implementation of a policy of hostages in concert with the Nazis.

Furthermore, economic repression, which was more insidious and even more dangerous than physical repression because of its capacity to wear down civilian populations, was carried out by the occupier. It involved stifling any leanings towards civilian resistance: by suspending the payment of salaries or dismissing staff in order to put an end to strikes, or by organising food shortages, the populations were gradually worn down, which drove them to direct all their attention towards finding food instead of taking action against the invader.

TRAGIC LOSSES FOR MIXED RESULTS

When the war ended in 1945, the death toll for members of the Resistance was high. In Poland, 100 000 people were dead and a further 50 000 had been imprisoned in the camps. In France, 20 000 people had been killed in combat, 30 000 had been shot, and over 60 000 had been deported, with almost half of them dying in the camps.

70 years after liberation, opinion is still divided as to the results that can be attributed to the actions of the Resistance. For the participants and some historians, the sacrifice was not in vain because it helped speed up the liberation of Europe by furthering the progression of the

heavy machinery of war through the finding of information and the organisation of acts of sabotage. However, others believe that the outcome of this action should be put into perspective in view of the number of people sacrificed for sometimes limited results. Nonetheless, however the military effectiveness of the Resistance, which did not have enough weaponry to secure victories, is viewed, its political action is unanimously considered to be positive in two countries. In France, members of the Resistance played an active part in organising the Normandy landings, notably thanks to information supplied to the Allies about Germany's military presence on the Atlantic coasts. They also played a decisive role in the Liberation of Paris. Finally, they successfully unified a population to prevent it from succumbing to the temptations of civil war and played a key part in the re-establishment of the Republic and the revival of French politics. In Yugoslavia, communist Resistance members led by Tito managed to liberate the country without the help of the Allies and the Red Army. Having secured this victory and the support of the population, in November 1945 they put in place a communist state, the Federal People's Republic of Yugoslavia.

In addition, transnational contacts established between different Resistance movements during the war led to the adoption of a *Manifeste de la Résistance Européenne* (Manifesto of the European Resistance) in Geneva on 20 May 1944. This text called for the creation of a federal union between the peoples of Europe. Its aim was to guarantee peace and allow economic reconstruction by putting an end to prewar nationalism and protectionism. Unfortunately, in concrete terms this manifesto was without consequence.

In any case, the fact remains that these men and women, who fought to try and put an end to the injustices of the occupation and the cruelty of the Nazis, can be considered true heroes.

SUMMARY

- On 1 September 1939, Germany invaded Poland, which brought Britain and France into the war against the Axis powers.
- During the first months of the war, the German army seemed invincible. It invaded Denmark, Norway, Luxembourg, Belgium, the Netherlands, France, Egypt, Yugoslavia and Greece before turning on its ally, the Soviet Union.
- The invaded countries were then occupied by the Germans, who imposed exceptionally difficult living conditions, characterised by shortages and fear.
- The governments of these countries then had two choices: collaboration with the enemy, the option chosen by Pétain, or resistance.
- Very quickly, different forms of civilian or organised resistance emerged across Europe. These networks would over time unify at the instigation of charismatic figures such as Charles de Gaulle and Jean Moulin in France.
- The actions of members of the Resistance, whether individual or in the form of popular gatherings, and whether they involved humanitarian activity, teaching or armed struggle, put them at risk of brutal repression from the German occupiers or collaborationist governments.
- Anyone who participated in the Resistance lived in constant fear of being discovered, arrested, tortured, imprisoned or executed, but also of causing the downfall of their network.
- Even today, opinion as to the results that can be attri-

buted to the actions of the Resistance remains divided. While some see the movement as having contributed to the success of several actions carried out by the Allies and as having enabled the re-establishment of democratic values, for others far too many lives were lost for the slight impact of their actions. Nonetheless, the fact remains that these individuals risked their lives fighting to protect liberty.

We want to hear from you!
Leave a comment on your online library
and share your favourite books on social media!

FIND OUT MORE

BIBLIOGRAPHY

- Bédarida, F. (1986) L'histoire de la Résistance. Lectures d'hier, chantiers de demain. *Vingtième Siècle*. Paris.
- Burrin, P. (1997) *La France à l'heure allemande. 1940-1944*. Paris: Seuil.
- De Rochebrune, R. and Hazera, J.C. (1995) *Les patrons sous l'Occupation*. Paris: Odile Jacob.
- Douzou, L. (2010) *La Résistance. Une morale en action*. Paris: Gallimard.
- Durand, Y. (1997) *Histoire générale de la Seconde Guerre mondiale*. Brussels: Complexe.
- Jacquemyns, G. and Struye, P. (2002) *La Belgique sous l'occupation allemande (1940-1944)*. Brussels: Complexe.
- Kershaw, I. (2008) *Hitler. 1936-1945*, Volume 2. Paris: Flammarion.
- Lehrman Institute (no date) *History*. [Online]. [Accessed 19 January 2017]. Available from: <http://lehrmaninstitute.org/history/index.html>
- Michel, H. (1972) *The Shadow War: Resistance in Europe 1939-1945*. Trans. Barry, R. New York: HarperCollins.
- Rings, W. (1982) *Life with the Enemy: Collaboration and Resistance in Hitler's Europe 1939-1945*. London: Weidenfeld & Nicolson.
- Rousso, H. (1992) *Les années noires. Vivre sous l'occupation*. Paris: Gallimard.
- Semelin, J. (1993) *Unarmed Against Hitler: Civilian Resistance in Europe, 1939-1943*. Westport, Connecticut: Praeger.

- Wywra, T. (1983) *La Résistance polonaise et la politique en Europe*. Paris: Éditions France Empire.

ADDITIONAL SOURCES

- Cobb, M. (2010) *The Resistance: The French Fight Against the Nazis*. London: Simon and Schuster.
- Gildea, R. (2016*) Fighters in the Shadows: A New History of the French Resistance*. London: Faber & Faber.
- Jackson, J. (2003) *France: The Dark Years, 1940-1944*. Oxford: Oxford University Press.
- Riding, A. (2012) *And The Show Went On: Cultural Life in Nazi-Occupied Paris*. London: Duckworth Overlook.
- Spotts, F. (2010) *The Shameful Peace: How French Artists and Intellectuals Survived the Nazi Occupation*. New Haven: Yale University Press.
- Vinen, R. (2007) *The Unfree French: Life Under Occupation*. London: Penguin.

ICONOGRAPHIC SOURCES

- Photograph of German troops entering Prague in 1939. Royalty-free reproduction picture.
- The 18 June appeal. Royalty-free reproduction picture.
- Photograph of de Gaulle's triumphant return to Paris, 26 August 1944. Royalty-free reproduction picture.
- Public notice announcing the measures taken to put an end to this resistance campaign in the Rouge Bouillon area of St. Helier, Jersey on 1 July 1941. Royalty-free reproduction picture.
- Photograph of Jewish prisoners reduced to slavery in

the Buchenwald concentration camp taken during the Liberation, 16 April 1945. Royalty-free reproduction picture.

- Photograph of a roundup during the Warsaw Ghetto Uprising. Royalty-free reproduction picture.
- Photograph of a woman having her head shaved in Montélimar, August 1944. Royalty-free reproduction picture.

IMPROVE YOUR GENERAL KNOWLEDGE

IN A BLINK OF AN EYE !

www.50minutes.com

www.50minutes.com

Ebook EAN: 9782806289872

Paperback EAN: 9782806293497

Legal Deposit: D/2017/12603/52

Cover: © Primento

Digital conception by Primento, the digital partner of publishers.